English Grammar Guide

to Accompany

¡Anda!

Donna Deans Binkowski

PEARSON

Prentice
Hall

woRLd
Languages

Upper Saddle River, New Jersey 07458

© 2009 by Pearson Education, Inc.
Upper Saddle River, NJ 07458

Printed in the United States Of America
10 9 8 7 6 5 4 3

ISBN 0-13-234435-1 / 978-0-13-234435-7

Table of Contents

1 Definite and Indefinite Articles

In English, we generally talk about three articles: *the, a,* and *an. The* is the **definite article,** used with nouns that refer to a specific person, place, or thing that is known to the speaker. *The* is used with both singular nouns, such as *boy* and *shirt,* and plural nouns, such as *houses*.

> *The* boy in *the* blue shirt is my brother.
> *The* houses on that street are all brick.

A and *an* are **indefinite articles,** used with nouns that do not refer to any specific item, but to one in a general class of items. *A* is used before words beginning with a consonant, such as *dog,* and *an* is used before those beginning with a vowel, such as *apple*.

> *A* dog ran across the road.
> *An* apple a day keeps the doctor away.

A and *an* are used only with singular nouns like *dog* or *apple*.

With plural nouns like *apples*, no indefinite article is needed, although *some* may be used.

> *Apples* are good for you.
> *Some* dogs ran across the road.

Got it?

1. Underline the definite article(s) in this sentence:

   We saw the boy leave the store.

2. Underline the indefinite articles(s) in this sentence.

   I lost a mitten and an earring in the snow yesterday.

2 Nouns

A **noun** is a word that names a person, place, or thing, such as an object, idea, animal, or event.

George Washington	-	person
Washington, D.C.	-	place
quarter	-	thing

A **proper noun** names a specific person, place, or thing, and begins with a capital letter in English.

<u>G</u>eorge <u>W</u>ashington
<u>W</u>ashington, <u>D</u>.<u>C</u>.
the <u>W</u>ashington <u>M</u>onument

A **common noun** names a general category of people, places, or things, and is not capitalized in English.

man	-	person
city	-	place
quarter	-	thing

Got it?

Label each noun **P** for "proper noun" or **C** for "common noun."

1. Mary
2. car
3. Manhattan
4. Niagara Falls
5. city
6. girls

3 Singular and Plural

Nouns in English can be classified according to their grammatical **number,** grouping them into one of two categories: **singular** and **plural.**

A **singular noun** refers to only one person, place, or thing.

 student
 watch
 mouse

A **plural noun** refers to more than one person, place, or thing. In English, to make a singular noun plural, we add -*s* or -*es*, although many nouns have irregular plural forms that must be memorized.

 student ⟶ student**s**
 watch ⟶ watch**es**
 mouse ⟶ mice

Got it?

Underline the plural noun(s) in this sentence:

 The students and teacher saw geese and ducks at
 the lake.

4 Adjectives

Adjectives are words that give more information about nouns. For example, in the phrases below, the adjective *blue* tells us more about the car, the adjective *big* tells us more about a house, and the adjective *sixteen* tells us more about the cats.

the car	⟶	the *blue* car
a house	⟶	a *big* house
cats	⟶	*sixteen* cats

In English, adjectives can generally be found immediately before the nouns they modify.

Adjectives in English have only one form, regardless of the number of the noun.

> This is my *favorite* book. (singular)
> These are my *favorite* books. (plural)

Got it?

Which of the following statements is true regarding adjectives in English?

- **a.** Adjectives agree with the noun they modify.
- **b.** Adjectives give more information about nouns.
- **c.** Adjectives are often found just before the nouns they modify.
- **d.** a & b
- **e.** b & c

5 Subjects

The **subject** of a sentence is the noun (or one of its substitutes) that performs the action described by the verb.

> *Kate* plays the flute.
> My *class* meets at 10:00.

If there is more than one verb in a sentence, each verb has its own subject.

These examples each contain two verbs and two subjects.

Kate plays the flute and *Mary* sings.

My *class* meets at 10:00, but today *I* am late.

Got it?

Underline the subject(s) in the following sentence:

Dad made coffee and Mom served the dessert.

 6 **Pronouns**

A **pronoun** replaces a noun when the noun has already been mentioned in the conversation.

John ate a whole pie. Now ~~John~~ *he* doesn't feel well.

Carla remembered Tom's birthday and decided to call ~~Tom~~ *him*.

In the examples above, a noun is replaced by a pronoun the second time it is mentioned.

A pronoun can also replace an entire **noun phrase** (a noun, together with its article and any adjectives that modify it). In this example, the pronoun *it* replaces the entire noun phrase *the big black dog*.

The big black dog looked fierce, but ~~the big black dog~~ *it* was really very playful.

Got it?

Which of the following statements is true?

a. A pronoun can replace a noun phrase.

b. A pronoun can replace a common noun.

c. A pronoun cannot replace a proper noun.

d. a & b

e. all of the above

6

7 | Subject Pronouns

A **subject pronoun** replaces a noun used as the subject of a verb.

> ~~Kate~~ *She* plays the flute.

There are eight subject pronouns in English:

	Singular	Plural
1st pers.	I	we
2nd pers.	you	you
3rd pers.	he, she, it	they

Subject pronouns are grouped by their grammatical number (singular or plural), as well as by person. **Person** is a grammatical term referring to the relationship of the pronoun to the people taking part in the conversation.

First person includes the speaker.

> *I* am speaking.
> *We* are talking on the phone.

Second person includes the listener but not the speaker.

> *You* are listening.
> *You* (plural) are talking.

And **third person** refers to other people.

> *He* is sleeping.
> *They* are leaving.

Got it?

Which of the following statements is true regarding subject pronouns in English?

a. Subject pronouns agree in number with the nouns they replace.
b. Subject pronouns agree in person with the nouns they replace.
c. Third person singular subject pronouns agree in gender with the nouns they replace.
d. all of the above
e. none of the above

8 Yes-No Questions

A **yes-no question** is one of the ways to ask questions in English. A yes-no question can be answered with a simple "yes" or "no." Yes-no questions often contain the words *do, does,* or *did*.

> ***Do*** you like apples?
> ***Does*** it rain a lot there?
> ***Did*** Kara get a good grade?

Other yes-no questions in English have this word order: *verb + subject*.

> ***Is she*** at the library?

Got it?

Which of the following sentences is an example of a yes-no question?

a. How are you today?
b. Do you know my sister?
c. Yes, I'll be there soon.
d. a & b
e. b & c

9 Making a Sentence Negative

Adding a negative word to a sentence changes the information that follows the word from true to false.

> Kate plays the flute.
> Kate does **not** play the drums.

> Tom is here.
> **No one** is here.

Notice that only the information <u>after</u> the negative word is false.

> Chris is a student and she is an athlete.
> Kara is a student but she is **not** an athlete.

The most common negative words in English are *not, no one, nobody, nothing,* and *never.*

Common negative words	
not	Kate does **not** play the drums.
no one/nobody	**No one** is here.
nothing	**Nothing** is on the table.
never	I **never** watch TV.

Got it?

What information is false in the following sentence?

I arrived late and did not take the test.

- **a.** I arrived late.
- **b.** I did take the test.
- **c.** a & b
- **d.** No information is false.

10 Question-word Questions

One way to ask questions in English is by using a **question-word question**. A question-word question is one that begins with an interrogative word. The most common interrogative words in English are *who, what, which,* and *how much/how many*.

Who asks a question about a person.

Who is she?

Other forms of *who* are *whom* and *whose*.

To **whom** am I speaking?
Whose child is that?

What asks a question about a thing.

What is it?

Which asks for a selection or choice and can be used with either people or things.

Which one is mine?
Which girl is your sister?

How much and *how many* ask for a quantity and can be used with either people or things.

How much does it cost?
How many students are there?

Got it?

Which of the following interrogative words can be used to ask questions about people?

a. what
b. how many
c. which

d. a & b
e. b & c

11 Verbs

Verbs are generally associated with action. They tell what is happening in a sentence.

> She *runs.*
> We *danced.*

Some sentences don't describe an action. In these sentences, the verb shows the state of mind or state of being of someone or something.

> I *am* happy.
> They *were* wet.

Got it?

Which of the following statements is true?

a. Verbs describe what is happening.
b. Verbs describe someone's state of mind.

c. Verbs describe a state of being.
d. all of the above
e. none of the above

12 Conjugation / Infinitive

The **infinitive** is the base form of a verb, the form that appears in the dictionary. All infinitives in English have the form *to + verb.*

> to go
> to ring

Conjugation is changing the form of the infinitive to agree with the subject and indicate the verb tense. For example, we can't say *He to go*. We have to conjugate the infinitive in the third person singular: *He goes*.

He to go. ⟶ He goes.

Each tense has six forms—one for each person and number.

	Singular	Plural
1st pers.	I	we
2nd pers.	you	you
3rd pers.	he, she, it	they

In English, many of the conjugations share the same form, so the subject must be mentioned with the verb for clarity.

to go	
I go	we go
you go	you (plural) go
he/she/it goes	they go

Got it?

Underline the conjugated verb(s) in the following sentence:

He likes to sing and he has a band.

13 Tense

Verb tense is the time at which the action takes place. We conjugate verbs in different tenses to indicate that something happened in the **past**, will happen in the **future**, or is happening now, in the **present**.

> I *ran* two miles.
> I *will make* an omelet.
> I *work* in the library.

In English, the past and present are simple tenses because they are made up of just one verb form.

> I *ran* two miles.
> I *work* in the library.

All the other tenses are compound tenses because they are formed by adding **auxiliary verbs** to the **main verb** form.

> I *will make* an omelet.
> It *was raining* earlier.

Auxiliary verbs are sometimes called **helping verbs** because they help to clarify the tense of the main verb.

Got it?

We conjugate verbs in different tenses to indicate that something happened. . .

  a. at a certain time
  b. to a certain person
  c. in a certain place
  d. none of the above

14 Present Indicative

The **present tense** is a verb conjugation that is used when the action of the verb takes place in the present.

> I *am* happy.

In English, it is also used for actions that happen on a regular basis and for stating general truths.

I **work** in the library.

Cars **are** expensive.

The term **indicative** refers to the grammatical mood of the verb. Indicative mood is used when the speaker considers something factual, certain, or objective.

The **present indicative** in English is a simple tense because it is made up of a single verb form, without auxiliary verbs.

Present indicative	
to run	
I run	we run
you run	you (pl) run
he/she/it runs	they run

For regular verbs, the present tense is formed by omitting the *to* of the infinitive. Only the third person singular requires an added final *-s*.

Since only the third person singular has a distinctive form in the present indicative, the subject must be mentioned with the verb for clarity.

to dance	
I dance	*we* dance
you dance	*you* (pl) dance
she dances	*they* dance

Got it?

Underline the present indicative verbs form(s) in this sentence:

I have a test today, so I studied all night.

15 Subject-Verb Agreement

When we conjugate a verb in English, we change the form of the infinitive to agree with the subject. **Agreement** is a grammatical concept meaning that related words have forms that match or go together.

There are rules about agreement in English. That's why a sentence like *I goes to school* is considered ungrammatical. The verb *to go* must be conjugated to agree with the subject *I*.

~~I goes to school~~. ⟶ *I go* to school.

Each tense has six forms—one for each person and number.

	Singular	Plural
1st pers.	I	we
2nd pers.	you	you
3rd pers.	he, she, it	they

Got it?

Which sentence illustrates correct subject-verb agreement?

a. He talk on the phone.
b. You works in the library.
c. They eat lunch together.
d. a & b
e. b & c

16 Idiomatic Expressions

An **idiomatic expression** is a phrase or group of words that means something different than the meaning of each of the words that makes up the group. For example, the meaning of the expression *to bury the hatchet* cannot be guessed from the meanings of *to bury* and *the hatchet*.

> to bury the hatchet   *bury + hatchet*

There are many colorful idiomatic expressions in English.

> She is not *playing with a full deck*.
> He is *in over his head*.

Idiomatic expressions are common in all languages, but they cannot be translated directly from one to another.

Got it?

Which of the following statements is true?

- **a.** Idiomatic expressions cannot be translated word for word.
- **b.** English does not contain many idiomatic expressions.
- **c.** To learn the meaning of an idiomatic expression, you must know the meaning of each word.
- **d.** a & b
- **e.** b & c

17 Possessive Adjectives

A **possessive noun** names the person to whom something belongs. Possessive nouns in English end in *apostrophe s* (*'s*) or *s apostrophe* (*s'*).

Mark**'s** computer is new.
The girl**s'** parents are professors.

A possessive noun can be replaced by a **possessive adjective,** which must agree with it in number. Third person singular forms must also agree in gender.

A singular possessive noun can be replaced by a singular possessive adjective.

Singular Possessive Noun →	Singular Possessive Adjective
1st person	my
2nd person	your
3rd person masculine	his
3rd person feminine	her
3rd person neuter	its

Plural possessive nouns can be replaced by plural possessive adjectives.

Plural Possessive Noun →	Plural Possessive Adjective
1st person	our
2nd person	your
3rd person	their

Mark**'s**	→	*His* computer is new.
The girl**s'**	→	*Their* parents are professors.

The possessive adjective always agrees with the possessive noun it replaces, regardless of the possession. For example, the possessive adjective *his* agrees with the noun it replaced, *Mark,* and not with the possession, *computer* or *computers.*

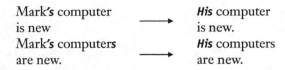

| Mark's computer is new | → | *His* computer is new. |
| Mark's computers are new. | → | *His* computers are new. |

Got it?

In English, a possessive adjective. . .

   a. agrees in number and gender with the possession.
   b. replaces a possessive noun.
   c. a & b
   d. none of the above

18   Auxiliary and Main Verbs

Some verb tenses, called **compound verbs,** are made up of two verbs: a **main verb** and an **auxiliary**—or helping—**verb.** The main verb is the one that describes the action, while the auxiliary verb tells when or how that action occurs.

   She can play the violin.
       | |
     aux. main

   She has run two miles.
       | |
     aux. main

In English, the most commonly used auxiliary verb is *to do,* which is used in the present and past tense to form questions and to express negatives.

   Do you study Spanish?
   Did you study last night?

I ***don't*** study Spanish.
I ***didn't*** study last night.

Other common auxiliary verbs in English include *can, has, is, will,* and *should.*

She ***can*** play the violin.
She ***has*** run two miles.
He ***is*** studying in the library.
He ***will*** get a good grade.
They ***should*** go to the grocery store.

Got it?

Underline the auxiliary verb(s) in the following sentence:

I don't have time today, but I can help you tomorrow.

19 Direct Objects

A noun or pronoun functions as an **object** when it tells who or what the action of the verb affects. A **direct object** is one that the verb acts on directly; that is, the effect of the action is felt directly by the direct object. We can find the direct object of a sentence by identifying the subject and verb and then asking *what?* or *whom?* after them.

In the sentence *Kara threw a ball,* we can identify *threw* as the verb and *Kara* as the one doing the action—that is, the subject.

Kara threw a ball.
| |
subj.   verb

If we then ask *Kara threw **what?,*** the answer is *a ball.*

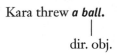

The same process works if the direct object is a person. In the sentence *Carla kissed John,* we can identify *kissed* as the verb and *Carla* as the subject.

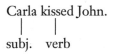

If we then ask *Carla kissed **whom?**,* the answer is *John.*

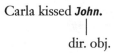

Some sentences contain more than one object, but only the object that is directly acted on is a direct object. For example, in the sentence *Kara threw a ball to her sister,* there are three nouns:

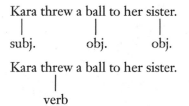

The verb in the sentence is *threw,* so to find the direct object, we ask *Kara threw **what?***

The answer is *Kara threw a ball.*

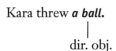

We know that *sister* is not a direct object because Kara did not throw her sister.

> Kara threw *her sister?*
> Kara threw *to* her sister.

Got it?

Underline the direct object(s) in this sentence:

> Chris gave her dog a bone.

20   Direct Object Pronouns

A pronoun replaces a noun when the noun has already been mentioned in the conversation. Just as a subject pronoun replaces a noun used as the subject of a verb, a **direct object pronoun** replaces a noun that functions as a direct object.

A noun or pronoun functions as an object when it tells who or what the action of the verb affects.

A direct object is one that the verb acts on directly; that is, the effect of the action is felt directly by the direct object.

> Carla kissed John.
> Carla kissed *whom?*
> Carla kissed *John.*
> |
>   dir. obj.

In English, three of the direct object pronouns are the same as the subject pronouns; five of them are different.

Subject pronouns		Object pronouns	
I	we	me	us
you	you (pl)	you	you (pl)
he	they	him	them
she		her	
it		it	

Direct object pronouns can also be distinguished from subject pronouns in English by their position in a sentence. Direct object pronouns in English always appear after the verb whose action they receive.

He called **her.**

Got it?

Which of the following pronouns can replace a direct object noun?

a. they

b. we

c. her

d. a & b

e. b & c

21 Demonstrative Adjectives

A **demonstrative adjective** is used to locate a noun in space and time. The four most commonly used demonstrative adjectives in English are *this, that, these,* and *those.*

This and *that* are used with singular nouns.

This car is new and **that** car is old.

These and *those* are used with plural nouns.

These leaves are red and **those** leaves are yellow.

This and *these* refer to nouns that are near the speaker, while *that* and *those* point to nouns that are farther away.

The distance indicated can also be in time.

> **This** summer seemed short compared to **those** summers when we were children.

Got it?

Match each picture with the appropriate demonstrative adjective.

1

2

3

4

picture 1 _____
picture 2 _____
picture 3 _____
picture 4 _____

a. this hat
b. that hat
c. these hats
d. those hats

22 Demonstrative Pronouns

A noun phrase that is made up of a demonstrative adjective and a noun can be replaced with a **demonstrative pronoun.** In English, demonstrative pronouns have the same form as demonstrative adjectives.

This and *that* replace singular nouns, while *these* and *those* replace plural nouns.

> I like **this ice cream!** ⟶ I like **this!**
> Did you win all
> **those medals?** ⟶ Did you win all **those?**

This and *these* replace nouns that are near the speaker, and *that* and *those* replace nouns that are farther away.

> **These** are new.
> **That** is old.

The distance can be in space or in time.

> **Those** were the days.

Demonstrative pronouns can also be used to refer to an idea or an unidentified object.

> Do you believe **that?**
> What are **those?**

Got it?

Match each picture with the appropriate demonstrative pronoun.

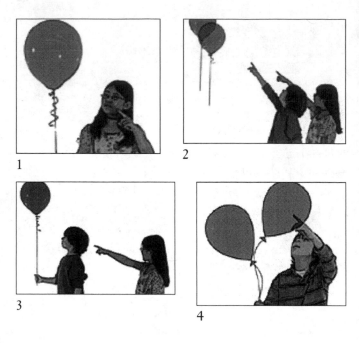

picture 1 _____   picture 3 _____   **a.** this   **c.** that
picture 2 _____   picture 4 _____   **b.** these   **d.** those

23 Neuter

Neuter is a grammatical term indicating that a word does not have a specific gender. The pronoun *it* is neuter in English. *It* is used to replace any noun that does not have a gender.

    I'll take this sweater. ⟶ I'll take *it.*

Most nouns in English do not have grammatical gender, but nouns that refer to people often refer to one gender.

Tom called *Carla.*
Carla called *her* son.

Nouns whose meanings imply a gender are replaced with the pronouns for that gender.

Carla called *her* son.

Sometimes we extend the use of pronouns that imply a gender to animals, especially pets.

Chris washed her dog. ⟶ She washed *him.*

All other nouns are considered neuter and can be replaced with *it.*

Mark washed his car. ⟶ Mark washed *it.*

Got it?

Which of the following nouns can be replaced by the neuter pronoun *it?*

a. my brother   **d.** a & b
b. my house   **e.** b & c
c. Jack

24 Subject / Object

The **subject** of a sentence is the noun (or one of its substitutes) that performs the action described by the verb. To decide which noun in a sentence is the subject, ask *Who + verb?* or *What + verb?*

For example, in the sentence *Mark plays the guitar for Chris,* we ask *Who plays?* The answer is *Mark. Mark* is the subject.

In the example *The hat is on the table,* we ask *What is?* The answer is *the hat. Hat* is the subject.

Other nouns or pronouns in the sentence may function as objects. An **object** is the person or thing affected by the action of the verb.

In our example sentence *Mark plays the guitar for Chris,* there are two objects: *guitar* and *Chris.*

Got it?

1. The following sentences contain four subjects. Underline them.

   My sister and I get up at 7:00. Mom makes breakfast and Dad reads the newspaper.

2. The following sentences contain three objects. Underline them.

   We have an exam tomorrow. We eat chocolate and listen to music while we study.

25 Reflexive / Non-reflexive Actions

An action is **reflexive** if the subject and object of the verb are the same. In other words, when the person doing the action and the person affected by the action are the same, that is called a **reflexive action.**

A reflexive action is expressed in English by adding a reflexive pronoun to the sentence. The reflexive pronoun agrees with the subject in person and number.

Reflexive pronouns	
myself	ourselves
yourself	yourselves
himself	themselves
herself	
itself	

He dresses *himself.*

Many verbs can function as either reflexive or **non-reflexive,** depending on the object. In the first example, *He dresses himself,* dresses is a reflexive verb because the object is the same as the subject. In the second example, *He dresses the child,* the subject and object are different. *Dresses* here, therefore, is not reflexive.

He dresses himself.
|
reflexive

He dresses the child.
|
non-reflexive

Got it?

Which picture illustrates a reflexive action?

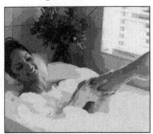 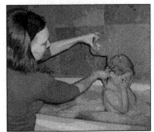

a. picture 1   c. both pictures
b. picture 2   d. neither picture

26 Reflexive Pronouns

Reflexive pronouns indicate that the object of the verb is the same as the person performing the action, the subject. Since the subject and the reflexive pronoun refer to the same person or thing, they will always agree in person and number

He dresses himself.

3rd pers sing., masc.   3rd pers sing., masc.

In English, reflexive pronouns end in -*self* in the singular and -*selves* in the plural.

Subject pronouns		Reflexive pronouns	
I	we	myself	ourselves
you	you (pl)	yourself	yourselves
he	they	himself	themselves
she		herself	
it		itself	

Many common verbs are reflexive.

The cat **bathes** itself.
The baby **feeds** herself.

In some cases, English omits the reflexive pronoun when the reflexive nature of the action is understood.

George shaves (himself).

Got it?

Which of the following statements is true?

a. Reflexive pronouns indicate that the subject and object are the same person.
b. Reflexive pronouns can be omitted in English sentences if the reflexive meaning is understood.
c. Reflexive pronouns are always plural.
d. a & b
e. b & c

27 Reciprocal Action

A **reciprocal action** involves two or more people (or things) who do things to or for one another. In other words, there are two subjects and each of them is the object of the other's action.

> Kara and Mark write to each other. = Kara writes to Mark and Mark writes to Kara.

The verb that expresses reciprocal action must be plural, since there are always at least two subjects performing the action.

> They write to each other.

Reciprocal action is usually indicated in English with the phrases *each other* or *one another.*

> We hug each other.

Got it?

Which picture illustrates reciprocal action?

a. picture 1
b. picture 2

c. both pictures
d. neither picture

28 Comparing Things That Are Equal

In English, when we compare two nouns that are equal in some quality, we use the phrase *as + adjective + as.*

George is **as strong as** Mark.

The adjective can compare any quality the two nouns have in equal measure.

Kara is **as old as** Chris.

The same construction can be used with an adverb in place of the adjective to compare how two actions are performed.

as + adjective + as
as + adverb + as

Chris runs **as fast as** her dog.

We can also compare equal numbers of things or people. The construction that expresses this is *as many + noun + as.*

Mark has *as many books as* Kara.
Tom has *as many students as* Karla.

Got it?

Which word or phrase could be used to make a comparison of equality?

  a. less hot
  b. as hot as
  c. hotter
  d. the hottest
  e. not as hot as

29 Comparing Things That Are Not Equal

In English, we have several expressions to choose from when we compare two things that are not equal. If we want to emphasize that one noun has less of a quality described by an adjective than another, we can use the negative form of the equal comparison *not as + adjective + as,* or we can use the construction *less + adjective + than.*

John is *not as tall as* Tom.
Kara is *less tired than* Chris.

In both cases, the noun that has less of the quality described is mentioned first.

If we want to emphasize that one noun has more of a quality than the other, we can use the comparative form of the adjective. For most adjectives, the comparative is formed by adding *-er* to the end of the adjective.

Tom is *taller* than John.

To emphasize that one noun has more of a quality than the other, we can also use the construction *more + adjective + than*.

Chris is **more tired than** Kara.

In both cases, the noun that has more of the quality described is mentioned first.

Tom is **taller than** John.
Chris is **more tired** than Kara.

Similar constructions are used for comparing unequal actions and unequal quantities of nouns.

Mark **studies harder than** George.
Kara **has more books than** Chris.

Got it?

Which phrase could be used to make a comparison of inequality?

- **a.** not as sick as
- **b.** sicker than
- **c.** as sick as
- **d.** a & b
- **e.** all of the above

30 Superlatives

When we compare two nouns, we can describe them as *more + adjective + than* or *less + adjective + than*.

Mark is **more studious than** George.

When we want to compare more than two nouns, we use the **superlative.** We can express the superlative by adding the suffix -*est* to the adjective or with the constructions *the most + adjective* and *the least + adjective*.

> George is ***the tallest.***
> Mark is ***the most studious.***
> Kara is ***the least studious.***

Some common adjectives, such as *good* and *bad,* have irregular superlative forms.

> Mark has the ***best*** grade.
> Kara has the ***worst*** grade.

Got it?

Which picture illustrates the superlative?

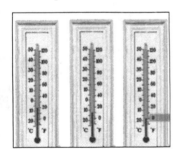   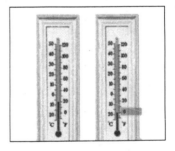

a. picture 1
b. picture 2
c. both pictures
d. neither picture

31 Present Progressive

The **present progressive tense** in English is formed by adding a present tense form of *to be* to the present participle (the *-ing* form) of the main verb.

He *is sleeping.*
They *are dancing.*

In English, the present progressive can indicate three things about the action it describes.

1. The action is in progress at this moment:

   He is sleeping.

2. The action is habitual:

   He is always playing tricks on his friends.

3. The action describes a general truth:

   She is studying to be a doctor.

Got it?

Which of the following sentences illustrates the present progressive?

- **a.** They run in the park.
- **b.** The used to run in the park.
- **c.** They are running in the park.
- **d.** a & b
- **e.** b & c

32 Present Participle

In English, the **present participle** is the verb form that ends in -*ing,* often referred to as the **gerund.**

> running
> talking
> eating

Present participles are used with the auxiliary verb *to be* to form progressive tenses.

> They *are eating.*
> We *were talking.*

They can also function as adjectives.

> They have a *talking* bird.

Got it?

Underline the present participle(s) in this sentence:

> We train every day because we're planning to run a marathon.

33 Indirect Objects

A noun or pronoun functions as an object when it tells who or what the action of the verb affects. A direct object receives the direct action of the verb, but an **indirect object** is one that the verb acts on indirectly.

We can find the indirect object of a sentence by identifying the subject and verb and then asking *to what?* or *to whom?* or *for whom?* after them.

> Chris gave a bone to her dog.
> Kara threw a ball to her sister.
> I bought my mom a necklace.

For example, in the sentence *Kara threw a ball to her sister*, there are three nouns:

the subject:	Kara
two objects:	ball, sister

The verb in the sentence is *threw*, so to find the direct object, we ask *Kara threw **what?*** The answer is *Kara threw a ball.* *Ball* is the direct object.

We know that *sister* is not a direct object because Kara did not throw her sister.

But if we ask *Kara threw **to whom?**,* the answer is *her sister.* *Sister* is the indirect object.

In English, either the word *to* or *for* is often found before the indirect object, but it is not required.

> Kara threw **to** her sister.
> I bought my mom a necklace.

Got it?

To find the indirect object of a sentence, we ask the question:

a. verb + what?
b. who + verb?
c. verb + to whom?
d. verb + why?
e. when + verb?

34 Indirect Object Pronouns

A pronoun replaces a noun when the noun has already been mentioned in the conversation. Just as a subject pronoun replaces a noun used as the subject of a verb, an **indirect object pronoun** replaces a noun that functions as an indirect object.

A noun or pronoun functions as an object when it tells who or what the action of the verb affects.

A direct object receives the direct action of the verb, but an indirect object is one that the verb acts on indirectly.

In English, the same object pronouns are used for direct and indirect objects.

Object pronouns	
me	us
you	you (pl)
him	them
her	
it	

Three direct and indirect object pronouns are the same as the subject pronouns. Five of them are different. In English, they can also be distinguished from subject pronouns by their position in a sentence.

Subject pronouns		Object pronouns	
I	we	me	us
you	you (pl)	you	you (pl)
he	they	him	them
she		her	
it		it	

Object pronouns always appear after the verb whose action they receive.

I bought my mom (her) a necklace.

Got it?

Underline the indirect object pronoun in the following sentence:

We made it for her.

35 Past Tense

Verb tense is the time at which the action takes place. We conjugate verbs in the **past tense** to indicate that something happened in the past.

The simple past is formed by adding *-ed* to regular verbs.

He cook**ed** all day.

Other verbs have irregular past tense forms. Irregular past tense verbs must be memorized.

I *ran* two miles.

Got it?

Underline the past tense verb(s) in this sentence:

Everyone ran to the car because of the rain.

36 Perfective / Imperfective Aspect

Perfective and imperfective aspects are opposite ways of considering actions or states of being. They are encoded within the verb tense used to describe the action or state.

The **perfective aspect** considers the verb as a completed whole. It focuses on the action or state of being as a single unit, from outside the timeframe during which it occurs.

> She **walked** home.

On the other hand, the **imperfective aspect** focuses on the action or state of being as ongoing, in progress, repeated, or habitual. Another way to think of this is to say that the imperfective aspect considers the verb from within the time during which it occurs.

> She **was walking** in the park.

In English, the difference between perfective and imperfective aspect can be illustrated by contrasting the differing views of an action expressed in simple past and past progressive.

> She walk**ed** home. ⟶ perfective
> She **was** walk**ing** through the park. ⟶ imperfective

Note that perfective and imperfective aspect should not be confused with perfect tenses. All verb tenses encode aspect.

Got it?

Underline the verb(s) that encode(s) imperfective aspect.

> I was watching TV when the phone rang.

37   Prepositional Phrases

Prepositions are words that convey relationships—usually in time or space—and answer questions such as *when?*, *where?*, or *how?*

when?	⟶	before
where?	⟶	in
how?	⟶	like

A **prepositional phrase** is made up of a preposition and the noun or pronoun that follows. This noun or pronoun is called the **object of the preposition.**

before bed
in class
like her

A prepositional phrase functions as an adverb when it modifies a verb, an adjective, or an adverb.

He watched TV *before* bed.
Tom is *in* class.
Kara's sister looks *like* her.

When it modifies a noun or pronoun, a prepositional phrase functions as an adjective.

The hours *between 2:00 and 4:00* AM are the darkest.
He wants a bike *like theirs.*

Got it?

Which of the following statements is true?

a. A prepositional phrase can modify a verb, a noun, or a pronoun.

  b. A prepositional phrase answers the questions *verb + to whom?* and *verb + to what?*

  c. A prepositional phrase always functions as an adverb.

  d. a & b

  e. b & c

38   Affirmative and Negative

Adding a **negative** word to a sentence changes the information that follows the word from true to false.

> Kate plays the flute.
> Kate does *not* play the drums.

A sentence is negative when it contains a negative word or expression.

> Kate does *not* play the drums.
> *No one* is here.

The opposite of negative is **affirmative.** A sentence is affirmative if it does not contain a negative word or expression.

> Kate plays the flute.
> Tom is here.

Got it?

Choose the affirmative sentence.

  a. We called but nobody answered.

  b. She is always cheerful.

  c. I'm not tired.

  d. They never worry.

42

39 Definite and Indefinite

Most of the words we use to describe people and things are **definite;** that is, they identify someone or something specific.

the boy
that dog

Sometimes, however, we may refer to people or things without mentioning any specific or definite example.

someone
something

The words we use in this context are called **indefinite** because they do not identify a specific person or thing. Indefinite expressions can refer to people, things, or a measure of time.

Indefinite expressions
some
something
someone
sometimes
always
also
either . . . or

Got it?

Underline the indefinite expression(s).

Someone always thinks of something fun to do.

40 Indefinite and Negative Expressions

Each **indefinite expression** has a corresponding **negative** form.

Indefinite	Negative
some	none
something	nothing
someone	no one
sometimes	never
always	never
also	neither
either . . . or	neither . . . nor

In English, only one negative expression is allowed in a clause.

I have done **nothing!**
No one saw anything.

If a sentence contains the word **not,** then an indefinite word is used after the verb, rather than a negative word.

I have **not** done **anything!**

Got it?

Choose the correctly formed English sentence(s).

- **a.** I didn't tell no one.
- **b.** Never go there again.
- **c.** Someone said there was nothing wrong.
- **d.** a & b
- **e.** b & c

44

41 Imperfect (Aspect)

We conjugate verbs in the past tense to indicate that something happened in the past.

The simple past, which is formed by adding *-ed* to regular verbs, indicates that an action was completed in the past.

> I work***ed*** all day.

When we describe something that *was happening* in the past, we focus on a point in time when that action was in progress. The verb forms we use to talk about such actions are called the **imperfect.**

In English, two constructions are used to express **imperfect aspect:** the **past progressive** and the phrase *used to.*

The past progressive is formed by adding *was* or *were* to the progressive (the *-ing* form of the verb). The past progressive describes what was happening during some time period in the past.

> I ***was*** sleep***ing.***
> They ***were*** study***ing.***

The phrase *used to* + *verb*—which may be stated or simply implied by the sentence—describes what used to happen in the past, focusing on the ongoing or repeated nature of the action. The phrase *would* + *verb* sometimes implies *used to* + *verb.*

> We ***used to*** swim every day.
> When we were kids, we ***would eat*** ice cream.

This construction is often used to describe states of being in the past as well.

I *used to* get nervous before a race.

Got it?

Which of the following statements expresses imperfect aspect?

- **a.** I was running as fast as I could.
- **b.** We used to get home from class earlier last year.
- **c.** I told him not to buy them.
- **d.** a & b
- **e.** all of the above

42 Ordinal Numbers

The numbers we use to count the size of a group are called **cardinal numbers.**

There are **24** candles on the cake.

Ordinal numbers refer to a position in a series. They are adjectives used to order things relative to one another. Ordinal numbers—like *first, second, third,* and so on—put things in order.

We are on the **second** floor.

Got it?

Underline the ordinal number(s) in the sentence.

My first class is at 9:00.

43 Impersonal Subjects

Every sentence in English must have a subject, but sometimes we don't want or need to specify a particular person.

Impersonal subjects such as *you, people,* or *they* can be used in place of specific subjects.

> *You* never see him in the summer.
> *People* say he's kind.
> *They* say it doesn't exist.

In more formal English, the impersonal subject *one* is used.

> *One* can't believe everything *one* reads.

Got it?

Underline the impersonal subject in the sentence.

> John told me they don't take checks there.

44 Passive Voice

In **active** sentences in English, the subject *performs* the action described by the verb.

> Chris washes the dog.
> | |
> subj. action

In **passive** sentences, the verb is in the passive voice and the subject *receives* the action rather than performing it.

The dog is washed by Chris.

    | |
   subj. action

In English, passive verbs have the form *to be + past participle*.

is washed
was broken

The person performing the action may be mentioned or omitted.

The dog is being washed.

Additionally, the person performing the action may be unknown, unimportant to the message, or omitted to make the message more impersonal or more indirect.

Roses were sent to Chris.
The window was broken sometime yesterday.

Got it?

Which of the following statements is true?

- **a.** In a passive sentence, the subject performs the action.
- **b.** In a passive sentence, the subject may be omitted.
- **c.** In a passive sentence, the subject receives the action.
- **d.** all of the above
- **e.** none of the above

45 Adverbs

Adverbs are words that give more information about verbs, adjectives, other adverbs, or clauses.

They answer the questions *how?*, *how much?*, *when?*, and *where?*

> She plays **well.**
> He cooked **a lot.**
> They arrived **late.**
> She put the dog **outside.**

Many adverbs in English are formed by adding *-ly* to an adjective.

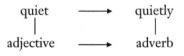

> He came in **quietly.**

Got it?

Underline the adverb(s) in the sentence.

> We arrived early, so we waited outside.

46 Subjunctive Mood

Indicative mood is used to indicate that what is being discussed is considered factual, certain, or that it can be objectively observed.

Subjunctive mood is used when the indicative is not appropriate; that is, when what is being discussed is not considered factual, certain, or objective.

In English, the subjunctive is often used to express wishes and formal requests.

>   I wish I *were* President.
>   They asked that everyone *take* a seat.

Wishes and requests express influence over someone or something else, or they express contrary-to-fact ideas.

>   I wish I were President (but I am not).
>   They asked that everyone take a seat (because they were standing).

Another common use of the subjunctive in English is the expression of hypothetical situations. Hypothetical situations do not describe something we have experienced, so they cannot be considered factual or certain.

>   If I *were* you (but I am not you), I would call her.

Got it?

Which of the following examples contains the subjunctive?

  a. I saw that he was smoking.
  b. We ask that you refrain from smoking.
  c. I wish he wouldn't smoke.
  d. a & b
  e. b & c

47 Noun Clauses

A **clause** is a group of words that contains a subject and a conjugated verb. A **noun clause** is a clause that functions as a noun in a sentence.

>   Whatever he does,...

A noun clause can function as the subject of the sentence, the direct or indirect object, or the object of a preposition.

> ***Whatever he does,*** she loves him.
> Do you know ***who called earlier?***
> They talked about ***what they should order.***

Got it?

Which of the following sentences contains a noun clause?

- **a.** What sets him apart are his good manners.
- **b.** I don't know him.
- **c.** Have you been there?
- **d.** a & b
- **e.** b & c

48 Independent / Dependent Clauses

An **independent clause,** sometimes called the **main clause,** expresses a complete thought. It does not require any additional words to form a complete sentence.

> We ate the cookies.

A **dependent clause,** sometimes called a **subordinate clause,** does not express a complete thought and cannot form a sentence on its own.

> she made

The dependent clause is added to the independent clause to form a sentence.

> We ate the cookies that she made.

Got it?

Which of the following clauses is an independent clause?

- **a.** he slept
- **b.** the class
- **c.** we liked
- **d.** all of the above
- **e.** none of the above

49 We Command (Let's)

The phrase *let's + verb* implies a command directed to others as well as to the speaker. This is called the **we command.**

> ***Let's go*** to the movies.

The main verb in the we command is in the infinitive form; it is not conjugated. The infinitive describes the action to be taken.

Often, this command is more of a suggestion or request than a direct order.

> "What do you want to do tonight?"
> "Let's go to the movies."
> "OK, but let's eat dinner somewhere first."

Got it?

Underline the we command in this sentence:

> We need to get some groceries, so let's stop at the store on the way home.

50 Indirect Commands

A **direct command** tells the listener to do something; it is a direct order.

> Go to the doctor.
> Feel better soon!

However, an **indirect command** expresses the speaker's hope that the listener will do something but does not directly order it. An indirect command may also tell the listener to allow or require someone else to do something.

> *Let* the doctor listen to your heart.

Got it?

Which of the following is an indirect command?

- **a.** Come with me.
- **b.** Go to sleep.
- **c.** Let him sleep all afternoon.
- **d.** Eat your soup.

51 Impersonal Expressions

Impersonal expressions convey opinions and beliefs about a situation as if they were general truths.

> It's important to take vitamins every day.

The subject of the impersonal expression is the situation it describes.

> It's a shame she couldn't come.

In English, impersonal expressions generally have the form *it's + adjective.*

> **It's impossible** to get through.

Got it?

Which of the following contain(s) an impersonal expression?

- **a.** I'm sorry you couldn't make it.
- **b.** It's great to see you!
- **c.** Let's get together again soon.
- **d.** a & b
- **e.** b & c

52 Commands

Commands, sometimes called **imperatives,** are orders someone gives to others to make them do something.

> **Go** to bed.

Commands can be distinguished from other verb forms in English because they use the infinitive form of the verb without *to,* and often without stating a subject.

> **Take** a message.

To make a command negative in English, we add *don't* before the verb.

> **Don't call** after 10:00.

Got it?

Which of the following is a command?

a. We should go home early.
b. He goes home early.
c. Don't go home early.
d. all of the above
e. none of the above

53 Conjunctions

Conjunctions are joining words. They join elements of a sentence to each other and indicate the relationship between them. **Coordinating conjunctions** join two equal elements, such as two nouns or two complete sentences.

> Mark *and* Kara
> dance *or* sing

Coordinating conjunctions in English include *and, but*, and *or*. Joining two sentence elements with a coordinating conjunction indicates that they are equal.

> Mark *and* Kara like to dance.
> Mark likes to dance, *but* George likes to sing.
> Carla can't dance *or* sing.

Subordinating conjunctions join a dependent clause to an independent clause.

Subordinating conjunctions in English include *because, if,* and *that*. Joining two sentence elements with a subordinating conjunction indicates that one is subordinate to the other.

> We can't go *because* of the rain.
> We can't go *if* it rains.
> I heard *that* it might rain.

Got it?

Underline the subordinating conjunction(s) in this sentence:

> The banks and post office were closed because of the holiday.

54 Adverbial Clauses

Adverbs are words that give more information about verbs, adjectives, other adverbs, or clauses. An **adverbial clause** is a dependent clause that starts with a subordinating conjunction—such as *although, because, when,* or *until*—and functions as an adverb.

Adverb clauses usually answer some question about the independent clause: *When? How? Why? Under what condition?*

> He watched TV *before going to bed.*
> Tom isn't happy *unless he is in class.*
> Kara's sister looks like her *even though she is much older.*

Got it?

Underline the adverbial clause in the sentence.

> We drank our coffee quickly although we weren't in any rush.

55 Past Participle

The present perfect and the past perfect are compound tenses because they are formed by adding a form of the auxiliary verb *to have* to the main verb.

> **have** + closed
> **had** + packed

The form of the main verb in the perfect tenses is called the **past participle.**

In English, the past participle of regular verbs is formed by adding *-d* or *-ed* to the infinitive.

close	⟶	close**d**
pack	⟶	pack**ed**

A number of other verbs form the past participle by adding *-n*.

give	⟶	give**n**

There are many irregular past participles in English, which have to be memorized.

do	⟶	done
leave	⟶	left
make	⟶	made

Got it?

Underline the past participle(s) in this sentence:

> I had forgotten our appointment, but we have scheduled another one for tomorrow.

56   Present Perfect Indicative

The **present perfect** is a compound tense formed by adding the present tense of the auxiliary verb *to have* to the past participle of the main verb. The present perfect often indicates that an action began in the past and is completed but still has some importance in the present.

> I *have finished* the book.

The present perfect may also describe actions that began in the past and continue in the present.

> He *has lived* here for two years.

Got it?

Which of the following sentences contains present perfect indicative forms?

- **a.** They had gone shopping.
- **b.** She has bought some books.
- **c.** We have eaten lunch already.
- **d.** a & b
- **e.** b & c

57   Past Participle Used as an Adjective

The form of the main verb in the perfect tenses is called the **past participle.**

> have + closed
> had + packed

The past participle can also function as an adjective when it is used to give more information about a noun.

58

In English, the past participle used as an adjective will generally precede the noun it modifies or follow the verb *to be*.

The **broken** window will be replaced.
The window is **closed**.

Got it?

Underline the present participle used as an adjective.

The spilled milk had covered everything.

58 Future Tense

In English, the **future tense** is a compound tense formed by adding the auxiliary verb *will* to the infinitive of the main verb.

I **will** wake up at 8:00.

In informal situations, the auxiliary *will* often forms a contraction with the subject pronoun.

I'll wake up at 8:00.

In very formal English, the auxiliary *shall* may be used in place of *will. Shall* does not form contractions.

I **shall** awaken at 8:00.

The future tense is used to describe actions that will take place at a later time.

I **will** wake up at 8:00.

Got it?

Which of the following sentences contains a future tense form?

   a. You will be late.
   b. I'll be early.
   c. We shall not arrive today.
   d. all of the above
   e. none of the above

59 Conditional Mood

The **conditional mood** is a compound verb form made up of the auxiliary verb *would* and the infinitive of the main verb.

   would be
   would like

The conditional mood is used to describe the result of a hypothetical situation; that is, what would happen if the hypothetical condition were met.

   If I were President, I **would balance** the budget.

Polite requests can also be formed using the conditional mood.

   Would you **pass** the salt, please?

Got it?

Underline the conditional verb form(s) in the sentence.

   If he ate the whole cake, he would get sick.

60 Imperfect Subjunctive

In English, the **imperfect subjunctive**, also called the **past subjunctive**, uses the same forms as the simple past. One exception is the verb *to be,* which uses the form *were* for all subjects.

> If only I *had* a new car.
> I wish it *were* summer.

Subjunctive mood is used when the indicative is not appropriate—that is, when what is being discussed is not considered factual, certain, or objective.

> If only I had a new car (but I don't).
> I wish it were summer (but it isn't).

In English, the past subjunctive is often used to express wishes and formal requests.

> I wish it were summer.

Another common use of the imperfect subjunctive in English is the expression of hypothetical situations.

> If it were summer, I would go swimming.

Got it?

Underline the imperfect subjunctive verb(s) in the following sentence:

> We would invite them to stay with us if we had more room.

61 Possessive Adjectives (Long Form)

To express possession in English, we often use short-form possessive adjectives, which appear <u>before</u> the possession and agree in number (and, in the case of the third person singular, in gender) with the possessor.

Short-form possessive adjectives	
my	our
your	your (pl)
his/her	their
its	

our house
her dog

Possessive adjectives also have a long form, composed of the phrase *of + possessive*.

Long-form possessive adjectives	
of mine	of ours
of yours	of yours (pl)
of his/of hers	of theirs
of its	

an old house ***of ours***
that dog ***of hers***

Note that the long-form possessive adjective follows the possession.

The long form of possessive adjectives may be substituted for the short form when we wish to emphasize the possessor rather than the possession.

her dog
that dog of hers

Got it?

Which of the following sentences contains a long-form possessive adjective?

- **a.** I lent her an old shirt of mine to paint in.
- **b.** We've decided to sell our house.
- **c.** I hope he finds his book soon.
- **d.** a & b
- **e.** b & c

62 If-clauses

If-clauses are clauses introduced by the conjunction *if*. They appear in hypothetical and contrary-to-fact statements.

> *If* it rains. . .
> *If* I had known. . .

A hypothetical statement describes something that could happen under certain conditions. The conditions are laid out in the if-clause.

> *If it rains*, we will not play today.

A contrary-to-fact statement describes something that has not happened because a certain condition has not been met. The condition is laid out in the if-clause.

> *If I had known she was coming,* I would have waited.

Note that the if-clause may precede or follow the other clause in hypothetical and contrary-to-fact statements.

If it rains, we will not play today.
We will not play today *if it rains.*

Got it?

Which of the following statements is true?

   a. If-clauses always begin hypothetical and contrary-to-fact statements.
   b. If-clauses describe conditions under which something could happen.
   c. If-clauses describe conditions not met in contrary-to-fact statements.
   d. a & b
   e. b & c

63 Hypothetical Situations

A situation is described as **hypothetical** if it has not happened but is viewed as possible.

   She would travel around the world.

A hypothetical statement describes a situation that occurs under certain conditions.

   She would travel around the world if she won the lottery.

Hypothetical statements are made up of two clauses: one which describes the hypothetical situation (1), and one which lays out the conditions under which the hypothetical situation could occur (2).

   (1) she would travel around the world + (2) if she won the lottery

The conditions are laid out in the if-clause, and the hypothetical situation is described in the result clause.

> She would travel around the world if she won the lottery.

Got it?

Which of the following is a hypothetical situation?

- **a.** if she were older
- **b.** we love to ski
- **c.** they can work together
- **d.** you would like it there
- **e.** it's always the same

64 Conditional Perfect

The **conditional perfect** is used as the past tense of the conditional. It is a compound verb form expressed by *would have + the past participle*.

> he **would have called** her

The conditional perfect is often shortened in informal speech, using a contraction such as *she'd*.

I'd	we'd
you'd	you'd (pl)
he'd/she'd	they'd

> **he'd have called** her

To make a conditional perfect verb negative, add *not* after *would*.

> we would **not** have gone

The conditional perfect is used to describe contrary-to-fact situations in the past.

> If he had gotten her number, he would have called her.
> If it had rained, we would not have gone.

Got it?

Which of the following verbs is in the conditional perfect?

  a. have been
  b. would enjoy
  c. would not have cared
  d. all of the above
  e. none of the above

65 Pluperfect Indicative

The **pluperfect indicative,** sometimes called the **past perfect indicative,** is a compound verb composed of the simple past of *to have* (*had*) and the past participle of the main verb.

> had finished
> had lived

In English, the pluperfect indicative indicates that an action was completed prior to another past action or point in time.

> I had finished the book.

In other words, it places an action at a point in the past longer ago than some other moment.

> He had lived here for two years before moving away.

Got it?

Underline the pluperfect indicative verb(s) in the following sentence:

John said he had written a novel.

66 Pluperfect Subjunctive

The **pluperfect**—or past perfect—**subjunctive** is a compound verb composed of the past subjunctive of *to have* (*had*) and the past participle of the main verb.

had been
had eaten
had passed

You may notice that the pluperfect subjunctive forms look just like the pluperfect indicative forms. It is the context that tells us if what is being described is indicative (considered factual, certain, or objective) or subjunctive (considered hypothetical by the speaker).

I was not hungry because I *had eaten* a snack.
If I *had eaten* a snack, I would not have been hungry.

In English, the pluperfect subjunctive replaces the imperfect subjunctive when the action described expresses the past tense.

If only it were summer.
If only it had been summer.

Got it?

Underline the pluperfect subjunctive verb(s) in this sentence:

I wish you had been home when we stopped by.

67 Adjective Clauses

An **adjective clause** is a dependent clause that functions as an adjective; that is, it gives more information about a noun.

The movie *that we saw* was funny.

In English, adjectives usually precede the noun they modify, but adjective clauses generally follow the noun they modify.

Adjective clauses can be introduced by relative pronouns, such as *which, that,* or *who,* but the relative pronoun may be omitted in informal speech.

The movie ~~that~~ we saw was funny.

Got it?

Which of the following contains an adjective clause?

a. the big blue balloon
b. the balloon that he bought
c. swimming all day
d. a & b
e. b & c

68 Relative Pronouns

Relative pronouns introduce dependent clauses that are used to give more information about the noun in the main clause. Dependent clauses that are introduced by relative pronouns are sometimes called **relative clauses.**

Kara, *who was running late,* missed the bus.

The relative pronoun is a pronoun because it replaces the noun from the main clause, avoiding repetition of the noun in the dependent clause.

> Kara was running late + Kara missed the bus   ⟶
> Kara, **who was running late,** missed the bus.

There are three main relative pronouns in English: *which, who,* and *that. Which* introduces relative clauses referring to things. Its form never varies.

> The bus, **which** comes at 8:00, didn't wait.

Who introduces relative clauses referring to people. Other forms of *who* include *whose* and *whom.*

> Kara, **whose** alarm was broken, missed the bus.

That may introduce relative clauses referring to either people or things. It's form is invariable.

> The new clock **that** Kara bought will work better.

Got it?

Choose the appropriate relative pronoun to begin each dependent clause.

1. The new teacher, _____ just started today, is nervous.

   a. which

2. Our house, _____ is white, needs new paint.

   b. who

3. My friend, _____ arm is broken, can't drive.

   c. whose

English Grammar Guide Answer Key

1.1 There are two examples of the definite article *the* in the sentence.

1.2 There are two indefinite articles in the sentence: *a* and *an*.

2. 1. **P**   2. **C**   3. **P**   4. **P**   5. **C**   6. **C**

3. There are three plural nouns in the sentence: **students, geese,** and **ducks.**

4. **e** Adjectives give more information about nouns, and they are often found just before the nouns they modify.

5. There are two subjects in the sentence (each verb has its own subject): **Dad** and **Mom.**

6. **d** A pronoun can replace a noun phrase, a common noun, or a proper noun.

7. **d** In English, subject pronouns agree in number and person with the nouns they replace, and third person singular pronouns also agree in gender.

8. **b** A yes-no question is one that can be answered with "yes" or "no."

9. **b** Only the information after the negative word *not* is false: I did *not* take the test, but I did arrive late.

10. **e** *How many* and *which* can be used to ask questions about people. *What* asks a question about a thing.

11. **d** Verbs describe actions, states of mind, and states of being.

12. There are two conjugated verbs in the sentence: **likes** and **has.**

13. **a** Verb tenses tell *when* something happened.

14. There is one present indicative form in the sentence: **have.**

70

15. **c** The verb form *eat* agrees with the subject *they.* In order to agree with the subject *he,* the verb form must be *talks.* In order to agree with the subject *you,* the verb form must be *work.*

16. **a** The meaning of an idiomatic expression cannot be guessed from the meanings of the individual words.

17. **b** In English, the possessive adjective always agrees with the possessive noun it replaces, regardless of the possession. In other words, a possessive noun can be replaced by a possessive adjective, which must agree with it in number and gender.

18. There are two auxiliary verbs in the sentence: *don't* and *can.*

19. *Bone* answers the question *What did Chris give?* The direct object is *bone.*

20. **c** *Her* is the only object pronoun. *They* is a subject pronoun. *We* is a subject pronoun.

21. picture 1: **b**   picture 2: **d**   picture 3: **a**   picture 4: **c**

22. picture 1: **a**   picture 2: **d**   picture 3: **c**   picture 4: **b**

23. **b** *My house* does not imply a gender and can be replaced by the neuter *it.*

24.1 The four subjects are *sister, I, Mom,* and *Dad.*

24.2 The three objects are *exam, chocolate,* and *music.*

25. **a** In picture 1, the woman is bathing herself. The subject and object are the same person, so this is a reflexive action.

26. **d** Reflexive pronouns indicate that the subject and object are the same person, and they can be omitted in English sentences if the reflexive meaning is understood.

27. **b** In picture 2, the elephants spray each other; this is a reciprocal action. In picture 1, the elephant sprays itself; this is a reflexive action.

28. **b** *As hot as* is used to make a comparison of equality. *Less + adjective* makes a comparison of inequality. *Adjective + -er* makes a comparison of inequality. *The + adjective + -est* is a superlative. *Not as + adjective + as* makes a comparison of inequality.

29. **d** Both *not as sick as* and *sicker than* could be used to make comparisons of inequality. *As + adjective + as* makes a comparison of equality.

30. **a** picture 1 We use a superlative when we want to compare more than two nouns. Picture 2 only compares two temperatures, so it illustrates the comparative.

31. **c** *They are running in the park* is an example of the present progressive. *They used to run in the park* is an example of the past. *They run in the park* is an example of the simple present.

32. There is one present participle: *planning.*

33. **c** To find the indirect object, we ask *verb + to whom?* or *verb + to what?*

34. The indirect object pronoun is *her.*

35. The past tense verb is *ran.*

36. *Was watching* encodes imperfective aspect. *Rang* encodes perfective aspect.

37. **a** A prepositional phrase can modify a verb, a noun, or a pronoun. It answers the questions *when?* and *where?* or *how?* An indirect object answers the questions *verb + to whom?* and *verb + to what?* A prepositional phrase can function as an adverb or as an adjective, but doesn't always function as an adverb.

38. **b** An affirmative sentence does not contain a negative word or expression. *Nobody, not,* and *never* are negative words.

39. There are three indefinite expressions: *someone, always,* and *something.*

40. **e** *Never go there again* and *Someone said there was nothing wrong* are correctly formed English sentences. *I didn't tell no one* is not, because in English only one negative expression is allowed in a sentence.

41. **d** *I was running as fast as I could* and *We used to get home from class earlier last year* express imperfect aspect. *I told him not to buy them* expresses completed action.

42. There is one ordinal number in the sentence: *first.*

43. There is one impersonal subject in the sentence: *they.*

44. **c** In a passive sentence, the subject receives the action and the person performing the action may be omitted.

45. There are two adverbs in the sentence: *early* and *outside.*

46. **e** In English, the subjunctive is often used to express wishes like *I wish he wouldn't smoke* and formal requests like *We ask that you refrain from smoking.* In option a, the indicative mood is used to indicate that what is being discussed is considered factual or certain and can be objectively observed.

47. **a** A noun clause must contain a subject and a conjugated verb but not be a full sentence.

48. **a** *He slept* is an independent clause. *The class* and *we liked* do not express complete thoughts and cannot form sentences on their own.

49. There is one we command in the sentence: *let's stop.*

50. **c** The other sentences are all direct commands.

51. **b** In English, impersonal expressions generally have the form *it's + adjective.*

52. **c** Commands, sometimes called imperatives, are orders someone gives to others to oblige them to do something. Only *Don't go home early* is a command.

53. There is one subordinating conjunction in the sentence: *because.*

54. There is one adverbial clause in the sentence: *although we weren't in any rush.*

55. There are two past participles in the sentence: *forgotten* and *scheduled.*

56. **e** Options b and c both contain present perfect indicative forms.

57. There is one past participle used as an adjective: *spilled.*

58. **d** All of the examples contain future tense forms.

59. There is one conditional verb form in the sentence: *would get.*

60. There is one imperfect subjunctive verb in the sentence: *had.*

61. **a** *Of mine* is a long-form possessive adjective. *Our* and *his* are short-form possessive adjectives.

62. **e** If-clauses describe conditions under which something could happen in hypothetical statements and conditions not met in contrary-to-fact statements. If-clauses may precede or follow the other clause in hypothetical and contrary-to-fact statements.

63. **d** *You would like it there* is a hypothetical situation that is dependent on some unstated condition. *If she were older* describes the condition under which a hypothetical situation could occur. *We love to ski, they can work together,* and *it's always the same* are statements of fact.

64. **c** Only *would not have cared* is conditional perfect. *Have been* is present perfect. *Would enjoy* is conditional.

65. There is one pluperfect indicative verb: *had written.*

66. There is one pluperfect subjunctive verb: *had been.*

67. **b** *The balloon that he bought* contains an adjective clause: *that he bought.* An adjective clause is a dependent clause that functions as an adjective.

68. 1. **b**   2. **a**   3. **c**